Contents

Introduction to the user

What is in the Video?

The Video contains four documentary sequences in which you see and hear real business people from around the world talking about and doing their work.

Sequence 1 Welcome to Arthur D Little (14 minutes)

In this sequence you visit a consultancy firm in the USA. You will see people:
- introducing themselves and their jobs
- using the telephone
- talking about numbers
- describing the company structure and areas of business

Sequence 2 Working for Volvo Car Corporation (13 minutes)

You visit the Volvo factory in Gothenberg, Sweden. You will meet employees:
- on the shop floor
- in the design department
- in administration
- in the health centre

You will see people talking about their work routines, likes and dislikes and making plans.

Sequence 3 At the London Boat Show (11 minutes)

You visit the factory where Fairline Boats are built. Then you see Fairline and Hunter Boats sales people at the Boat Show talking to customers and describing their product range.

Sequence 4 A business trip to Kuala Lumpur (12 minutes)

You visit Malaysia with a British business woman, Deborah Wildridge. You follow all the stages of the business trip:
- booking flight tickets
- checking in to a hotel
- visiting a factory
- touring the city

You also learn a little about Malaysia's economic development.

How can the Video help improve my English?

Working with the Video and this Activity Book, you will:
- practise listening to authentic Business English
- build your Business English vocabulary
- consolidate your English grammar

The Activity Book is designed to help you work with the Video on your own either at home or in a self-study centre. It prepares you for watching the Video, checks your understanding and gives you follow-up language practice. At the end of the book you will find answers to all the exercises and the video tapescripts.

There are basically five stages in the Activity Book for each part you watch:

1 **Preview:** this can be a vocabulary check or short reading. It prepares you for watching the Video. Occasionally we suggest you watch the part of the Video without sound first.
2 **First view:** this gives you a general understanding of the part.
3 **Second view:** this gives you a more detailed understanding of the part. Occasionally there is just one Viewing task for a part.
4 **Language work and Practice:** this is follow-up work to the viewing.
5 **Remembering key vocabulary:** this helps you record the important vocabulary.

Using the Answer Key with tapescripts

Problems?
When you have done an exercise, look at the tapescript in the Answer key. What did you have a problem understanding? Was it vocabulary or pronunciation? Analysing this will help you understand better in the future.

New vocabulary
Choose a few useful expressions each time and make a note of them.

Revision
Next time you watch, take your vocabulary list, repeat the last part you saw and tick (✓) your words and expressions as you hear them.

Some suggestions for working on your own

1 All four sequences are divided into small parts. Start by working on just one or two parts at one time.
2 Don't try and understand every word you hear. Answer the questions in the book which are designed to help you understand the important information.
3 Don't forget to use the pictures to help you understand what people are saying.
4 Use the numbers on the screen to help you work with the Video.
5 Do regular revision sessions. Before you start a new part, look again at the last part you worked on.
6 Use a bilingual dictionary to help you translate words.

1 Welcome to Arthur D Little

Introduction

Arthur D Little is a **consultancy** firm. Their job is to **give advice** to other firms. Companies contact them if they need help with a particular problem or if they need advice about starting to do business in a new area.

Thinking point: Do you know a company which has used a consultant? In what circumstances?

The sequence lasts 14 minutes and is organised like this:

Part 1   Registering at reception (00:24)

Preview
Guess the story.

Turn the sound off and watch to 01.08.

- What is the situation?
- What words or expressions do you expect to hear?

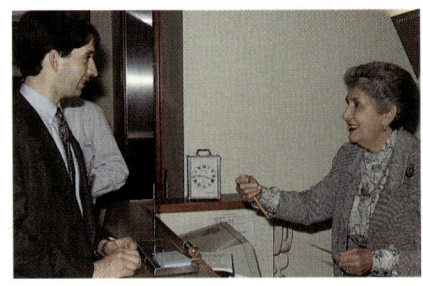

First view

**Read these questions. Then watch and answer these questions.
Are the statements true or false?**

1 Todd Rhodes is at ADL to see Tony Martrom.
2 His appointment is at 9.30.
3 The receptionist gives Todd Rhodes a badge to wear.

Second view

Watch again and answer these questions.

1 Does Thalia Skoulos, the receptionist, know Todd Rhodes?

....

2 Is she friendly to Todd Rhodes?

....

3 What does she ask Todd to do?

....

Language work

**These sentences come from the sequence.
Can you put the words in the right order?**

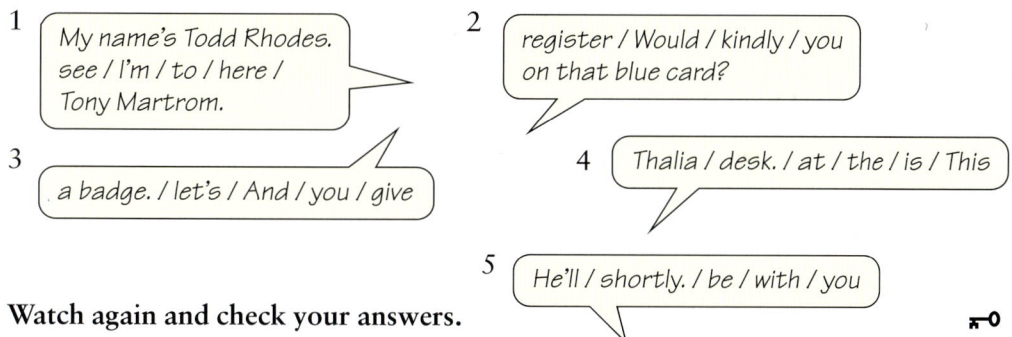

1
My name's Todd Rhodes.
see / I'm / to / here /
Tony Martrom.

2
register / Would / kindly / you
on that blue card?

3
a badge. / let's / And / you / give

4
Thalia / desk. / at / the / is / This

5
He'll / shortly. / be / with / you

Watch again and check your answers.

Remembering key vocabulary

**When you have corrected your work and looked at the tapescript, note about five
words or expressions that are important to you in the space provided.**

nouns	verbs	expressions

Revise these words later by watching the sequence again and ✓ ticking the words
as you hear them. Try to remember the words in their context.

Part 2 An overview of the business (01:13)

2.1 The main business areas (01:20)

Ranganath Nayak talks about the company's
main business areas. It is quite a long part.
Don't try to remember everything. Just answer
the questions.
Note at ADL the word *directorate* means
division or *section*.

Preview

**Check the meaning of these words and
expressions in a bilingual dictionary.**

1 research and development   4 safety
2 environment   5 solve a problem
3 health

Now put them in the sentences which follow.

A At the end of the twentieth century most governments want to protect the

   ....

B The .... part of a company is responsible for finding new ideas and
   ways of working.

C Before he could start work he had a medical examination to show that he was in
   good ....

D A company employs a consultant to help them ....

E They checked the .... of all the machines in the factory.

Note that *go global* means to *become international*.   ⚷

First view

Read the question and then watch.

How many business areas are there? One, two or three?   ⚷

Second view

Watch again and complete the paragraph.

The first business area is research and product development (R&D) for companies. This is done in
Cambridge, Massachusetts, in the [1] T...................... and [2] P...................... Development
Directorate and in Cambridge, England, at Cambridge [3] C...................... Limited.

The second business area is Environmental, Health and [4] S...................... Consulting.

The third area of business is [5] M...................... Consulting, for example how to enter the
[6] C...................... market.

Language work

Now try this puzzle.

Find five words from the interview in this grid.

a	n	r	d	m	a	n	a	g	e	m	e	n	t
r	w	u	o	v	d	u	t	o	e	o	d	e	p
e	q	r	y	u	v	c	e	l	b	d	n	u	r
s	w	r	i	t	e	l	a	q	o	p	c	e	o
e	w	t	m	c	c	i	k	h	s	i	o	e	d
a	w	t	q	z	h	e	z	x	k	e	l	c	u
r	h	o	e	n	r	n	e	y	p	h	j	s	c
c	o	n	s	u	l	t	i	n	g	e	y	o	t
h	p	w	u	a	h	o	d	n	e	e	t	e	s

Further practice

Write a paragraph about this company.

```
New Jersey Books
Based in New York
2,005 employees
Established in 14 countries
Turnover $504 million
Areas of business: magazines and books (worldwide) music
(Europe) videos (Europe and the USA)
```

- **Alternatively, write about a company you know.**

2.2 The size of the business (02:53)

Preview

1 The amount of money a company makes during a certain period is its
   ˙t...................o.................... .
2 Say the following numbers out loud:
   1,600   one <u>thous</u>and six <u>hun</u>dred
   $^1/_2$ a <u>half</u> /hɑːf/
   50 to 60   <u>fif</u>ty to <u>six</u>ty
3 Check the meaning of *roughly*, *over* and *approximately* in your dictionary.
   Now make sentences.
   .52 is roughly ....
   1,505 is ....
   2,001 is ....

First view

Read the following sentences and then listen to Ranganath Nayak talking about the size of the company. Fill in the gaps in the sentences.

1 The number of employees altogether in ADL: about ....
2 The number of cities where ADL has offices: .... to ....
3 The number of employees who are consultants: about ....
4 The turnover per year: about $................... .

Second view

Read these questions and then watch again.

1 % of employees who work in the USA: ....
2 number of offices in the USA: ....
3 Did Ranganath mention all the cities they have offices in?   ⚷

Language work

Complete this description of ADL.   ⚷

> ADL is in the [1] c................... business. It advises companies about their business in
> [2] t................... main areas: [3] R................... and Development; Environmental,
> [4] H................... and Safety; [5] M................... consultancy.
> ADL employs about 2,600 people and has offices all over the [6] w................... Its
> [7] t................... is roughly $300 million a year. Its [8] h................... are in Cambridge,
> Massachusetts, USA.

Remembering key vocabulary

When you have corrected your work and looked at the tapescript, note the words that are important to you in the space provided.

nouns	verbs	expressions about quantity

Revise these words later by watching the sequence again and ✓ ticking the words as you hear them. Try to remember the words in their context.

Part 3   Meet some people in the company (04:19)

Preview

Check the meaning of the words in the left hand column in your dictionary.
Then match these words with the definitions on the right.

1	strategy	A	going out
2	printing	B	putting papers together
3	binding	C	copying letters or pictures
4	freight (pronounced /freɪt/)	D	plan
5	inbound	E	goods to transport
6	outbound	F	coming in

First view

Match the people to their jobs or job titles.

1	Rana Gupta	A	a secretary.
2	Ranganath Nayak	B	a Vice President and Managing Director.
3	Donna DeDomenico	C	the traffic manager.
4	Joe Bottari	D	a Human Resources Manager.
5	Mary Janaitis	E	a Laboratory Supervisor.
6	Carl Johnson	F	the supervisor of the print shop.
7	Melissa Rigatti	G	a consultant.
8	Connie Coppinger	H	a Support Staff Administrator.

is

Listen again. Who said …?

1 I'm a member of the management committee here.

2 I do a wide range of things.

3 I'm involved in all aspects of moving freight.

4 People have trouble with my whole name.

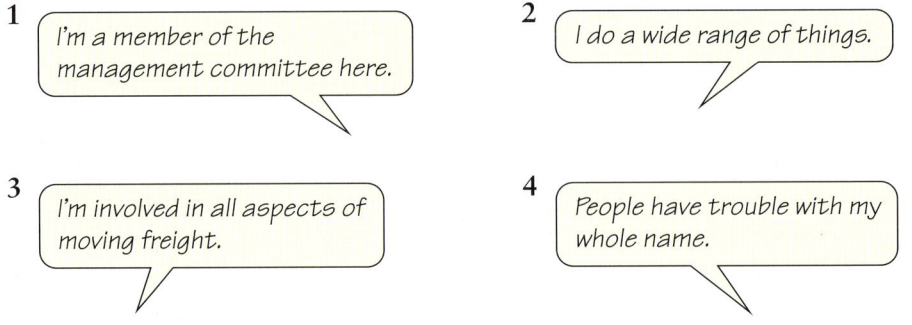

Language work

Look at these words from the interview. Which syllable is stressed? The first one has been done for you.

1 con<u>sul</u>tant   5 resources
2 management   6 deliveries
3 secretary   7 laboratory
4 supervisor   8 environmental

Remembering key vocabulary

When you have corrected your work and looked at the tapescript, note the words that are important to you in the space provided.

management jobs	other types of jobs

Revise these words later by watching the sequence again and ✓ ticking the words as you hear them. Try to remember the words in their context.

Part 4 Behind the scenes (07:15)

4.1 In the Copy Center (07:20)

Preview

Question: What is ADL's main product? 🔑

Check these words in your
dictionary and add any other types
of business documents you know.

reports
proposals
brochure
internet news
e-mail

First view

Listen to Joe Bottari
and answer this
question. What is
happening in the
photos? 🔑

1 p................................

2 p................................

3 b................................

Second view

Tick the documents Joe Bottari talks about.

reports   catalogues
proposals   factsheets
brochures   letters
memos   faxes   🔑

4.2 On the phone (08:03)

Preview

What do you say
1 when you pick up the phone?
   ".."

2 when you transfer a call?
   ".."

3 when you finish a call?
   ".."

First view

Listen to Donna DeDomenico on the phone.

Does Donna a) transfer the call or b) take a message?

Second view

Put these sentences in the right order. (The first and the last sentences are correct.)

Environmental Management, Donna speaking.	1
A Very good. I'll have him call you back.	......
B OK. OK. And your phone number there, please?	......
C Could I have him call you back?	......
D And can you spell that, please?	......
E I'm sorry he's not in the office right now.	......
You're welcome. Bye bye.	7

• **Listen again. Were you correct?**

Language work

Now write down what you think the caller says.

DONNA: Environmental Manager, Donna speaking.
CALLER: ....
DONNA: I'm sorry he's not in the office right now. Could I have him call you back?
CALLER: ....
DONNA: And can you spell that please? OK. OK.
CALLER: ....
DONNA: And your phone number there, please?
CALLER: ....
DONNA: Very good. I'll have him call you back.
CALLER: ....
DONNA: You're welcome. Bye bye.

Remembering key vocabulary

When you have corrected your work and looked at the tapescript, note six words that are important to you in the space provided.

nouns	verbs	telephone expressions

Revise these words later by watching the sequence again and ✓ ticking the words as you hear them. Try to remember the words in their context.

Part 5   The Technology and Product Development Directorate (08:46)

5.1 Working with the food industry (08:55)

Preview

Check the following words in
your dictionary.

background (of a person)
ingredient
PhD

First view

Watch this section. Correct this information
on Gail Greenwald's career resumé (c.v.). ⚏O

<u>Career resumé</u>
<u>Present position</u>
Senior Vice President and Associate Director
at ADL
<u>Specialty</u>
Food preservatives and ingredient technology.
<u>Background</u>
PhD in biological engineering
I have worked at ADL for 14 years.

Second view

Listen to Gail Greenwald talking in the laboratory, and fill in the missing words. 🔑

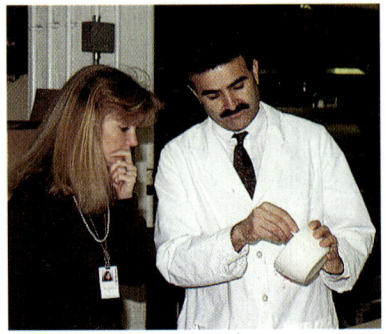

> [1] .... is Vanick Petrossian, [2] .... is one of our senior people in product development in the food [3] .... Today we're working on a mixture of fruits which we're using as base in a new [4] ....

Language work

Write a paragraph about yourself or someone you know using this model. 🔑

My name is ....
I'm a .... (job or position)
in .... (company).
I have .... (qualifications).
I specialise in ....

5.2 Two examples of product development (10:00)

Preview

Check these words in your dictionary.

main areas
lively
compete / competitive
rugged

First view

Listen to David Lee.
What two products does he talk about? 🔑

Second view

Listen again to David Lee and answer these questions.

1 What is the pencil made of?

2 What is special about this bike?
   A its weight   B its colour   C its price   D its speed   🔑

Language work

Read the tapescript on page 57 and find words with these endings. Also, add your own words that end like this.   ⌐○

-ical   -tion   -logy
chemical

Now mark the stress on the words like this: <u>chem</u>ical. Can you see a rule for pronunciation?

Remembering key vocabulary

When you have corrected your work and looked at the tapescript, note six words that are important to you in the space provided.

nouns	verbs	expressions

Revise these words later by watching the sequence again and ✓ ticking the words as you hear them. Try to remember the words in their context.

Part 6   The Environmental, Health and Safety Directorate (11:19)

Preview

Important vocabulary in this part.

landfill = an area of waste ground where rubbish is buried
to audit = to check
to set up = to establish

Why might the owner of a landfill site consult ADL?   ⌐○

First view

Listen to Anthony Hyde, a senior consultant in the EHS directorate, talk about his work and answer these questions.

1 What kind of problem does he help with?
2 Where does he spend his time abroad?

Second view

Read this transcript and pencil in the appropriate words in the gap.

Most of my working [1] l......... is spent helping [2] p................. solve [3] p.................
with [4] e................., [5] h................., or safety concerns. A lot of my
[6] t................. is spent [7] a................., a lot of the time in the Far East,
[8] w.................ing with clients [9] d.................ing safety auditing,
[10] s.................ing up safety management [11] s................. and that sort of thing.

• Now watch again and check your answers.

Remembering key vocabulary

When you have corrected your work and looked at the tapescript, note six words that are important to you in the space provided.

nouns	verbs	expressions

Revise these words later by watching the sequence again and ✓ ticking the words as you hear them. Try to remember the words in their context.

Part 7   The Management Consultancy Directorate (11:58)

7.1   The Management Consultancy's clients (12:06)

Preview

Check the meaning of **management consultancy** in your dictionary.
Have you had any experience of working with management consultants?
When do companies use them?

First view

**Karl Loos is a Senior Vice President
at ADL. Listen to him talking about
management consultancy at ADL.** 🔑

How many industries does he mention?
A eight
B nine
C ten

Second view

Tick the industries Karl Loos mentions.

☐ chemicals   ☐ pulp and paper   ☐ automotive
☐ energy   ☐ banking   ☐ aerospace
☐ publishing   ☐ metals   ☐ information systems
☐ pharmaceuticals ☐ oil   🔑

7.2   How the Management Consultancy Directorate is organised
            (12:36)

Preview

Important vocabulary in this part.

boundary = dividing line between two pieces
segment = part

Complete the following sentences with either boundary **or** segment.

1 For many years the company dominated that .... of the market.
2 The river is the .... between the two countries.   🔑

First view

Listen to Karl Loos. How many geographic segments are there to the MCD? 🔑

Second view

In the ADL brochure there is a map showing their business areas. Which map is it?

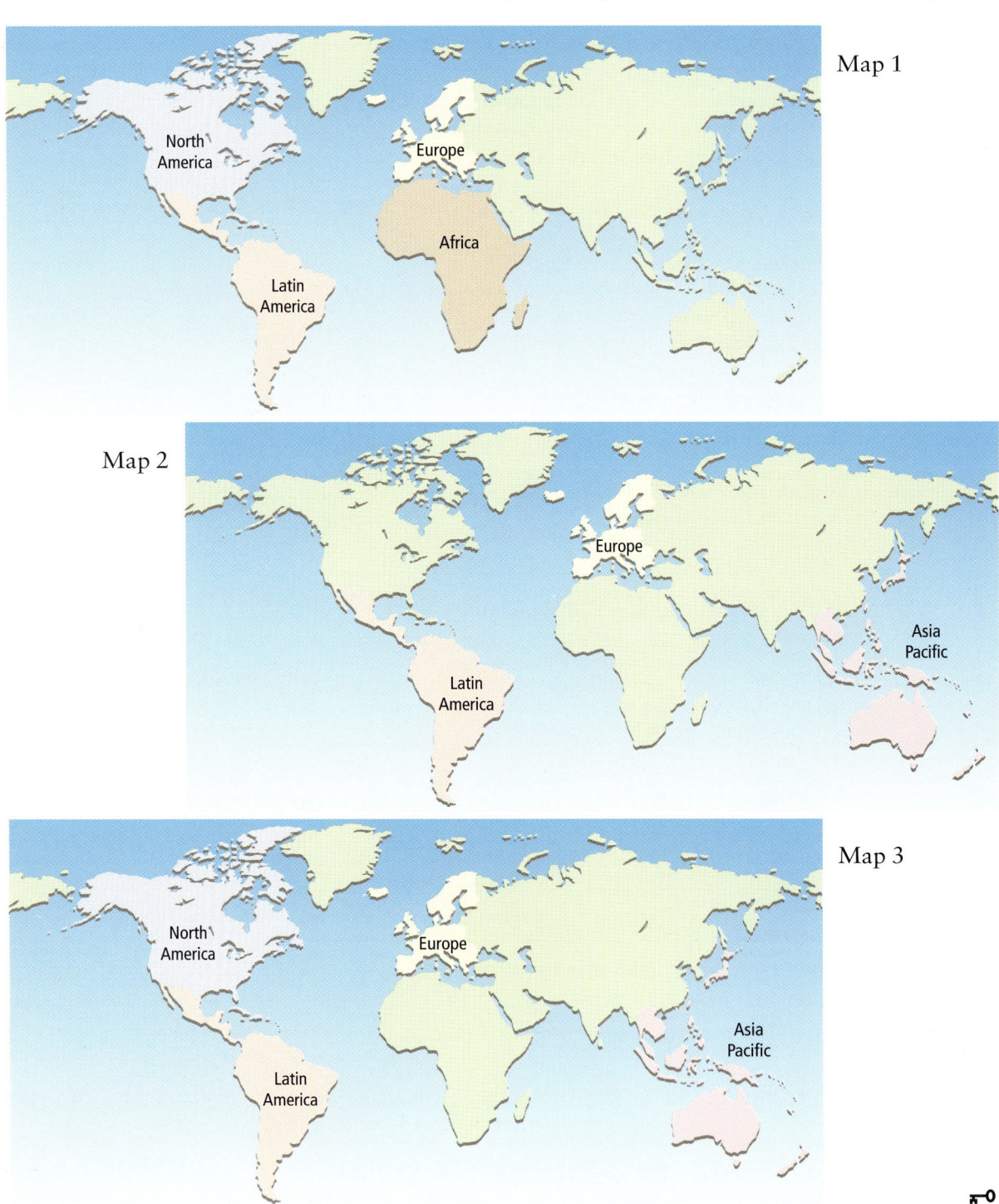

Part 8   ADL – the perfect partner? (13:00)

Preview

Check the meaning of these words in your dictionary.

broad   span
complete   range of services

First view

In this part Ranganath Nayak explains why he thinks ADL is the perfect partner.

Many management consultants
do environmental and technical work.
True or false?

Second view

**Explain in your own words
why Ranganath Nayak thinks
you should choose ADL.
This diagram may help you
to answer the question.**

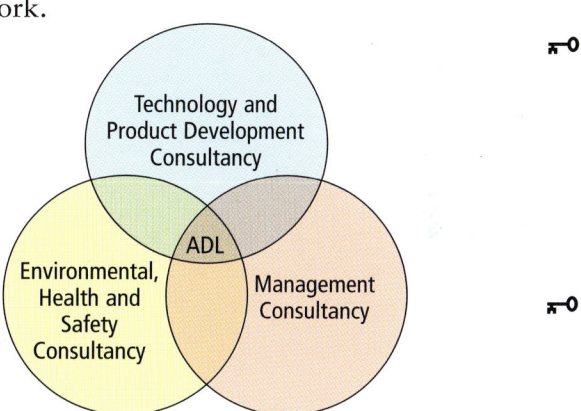

Remembering key vocabulary

**When you have corrected your work and looked at the tapescript, note six words
that are important to you in the space provided.**

nouns	verbs	expressions

Revise these words later by watching the sequence again and ✓ ticking the words
as you hear them. Try to remember the words in their context.

2 Working for Volvo Car Corporation

Introduction

In this sequence you visit the headquarters of Volvo in Gothenburg, Sweden. 🔑

- What do you know about Volvo?
- What sort of vehicles do they manufacture?
- How would you describe a Volvo car?
- What is Volvo famous for?

Now read this and see if your answers were right.

VOLVO

We have 63,600 employees worldwide and sales of $13,716 million. We manufacture cars, trucks, buses and marine and industrial engines. We also work in the aerospace industry. Our position as a major international group with large operations in Europe and North America is a result of quality, safety and caring for people and the environment.

The sequence lasts 13 minutes and is organised like this:

Part 1	Talking about your work
Part 2	Routines
	2.1 In the factory
	2.2 In the offices
Part 3	Travel
	3.1 Kerstin Malmgren's travel plans
	3.2 The Monte Carlo seminar schedule
Part 4	Likes and dislikes
Part 5	Stress
	5.1 Dealing with stress
	5.2 Leisure activities
Part 6	Working atmosphere and company culture

Introduction to the video (00:00)

Watch from the beginning to 00:29. Which of the following things do you see?

1 a black car by the sea ☐
2 a rally driver in a Volvo ☐
3 people building a car ☐
4 a yellow car on the open road ☐
5 robots building a car ☐
6 a computer simulation of a crash ☐
7 a couple driving a car ☐
8 safety testing of a car ☐
9 a car in traffic ☐
10 the steering wheel of a car ☐

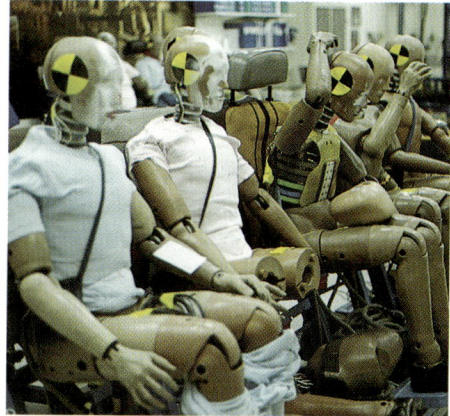

Part 1 — Talking about your work (00:29)

Preview

Match the parts of the plant with their activities. Check any words you are not sure of in your dictionary.

Parts of the plant
1 The body shop
2 The paint shop
3 The assembly line
4 The health and fitness centre   is
5 The public relations (PR) department
6 The design centre

Activity
A where people go to play sport and to exercise.
B where the engine and seats are put in.
C where the shell of the car is made.
D where the car is painted.
E where the shape and style of future cars are planned.
F the part of the company which makes sure the company has a good image to the outside world.

First view

Watch this part and match the people to their departments.

1	Birgitta Hopkins		A	the assembly plant.
2	Christer Weiss		B	the health and fitness centre.
3	Lisa Nyberg	works in	C	the body shop.
4	José L. Diaz de la Vega		D	the public relations department.
5	Kerstin Malmgren		E	the design department.

Second view

Complete these sentences.

1 Birgitta Hopkins and her colleagues produce the roof, the .... and the sides of the car.
2 Christer Weiss's responsibility is to .... engines.
3 People come to see Lisa Nyberg for ....
4 José L. Diaz de la Vega says design is a .... tool.
5 Kerstin Malmgren works in .... at the moment, but will move back to Sweden in ....

Language work

Read the tapescript on page 59/60 and find words which mean:

Birgitta

enough ....
make ....

Christer

assemble ....

Lisa

the majority ....

José

What's your opinion? ....
....
someone who buys ....

Kerstin

at the moment ....

Remembering key vocabulary

When you have corrected your work and looked at the tapescript, note six words that are important to you in the space provided.

nouns	verbs	expressions

Revise these words later by watching the sequence again and ✓ ticking the words as you hear them. Try to remember the words in their context.

Part 2 Routines (03:10)

2.1 In the factory (03:17)

Preview

Read the following.

> The work in the factory is divided into two *shifts*. Early *shift* is from 07.00 to 16.00; late *shift* is from 16.00 to 01.00.

What do you think *shift* means? If you are not sure check the meaning in your dictionary but be careful as *shift* has several meanings.

What's your routine?

First view

Listen to Birgitta and Christer talking and answer these questions.

1 How many shifts are there: two or three?
2 How many coffee breaks are there?
3 How long is their lunch break: 40, 45 or 55 minutes?
4 How many days' holiday do they have: 20, 25 or 30?
5 Why does Birgitta like the late shift?

Second view

Listen again and fill in the table.

Birgitta's working week

	number of days worked	start	finish
early shift			
late shift			

Christer's working week

	start	finish
day shift		⟋
night shift		⟋

⌐O

2.2 In the offices (04:46)

First view

Listen to Kerstin, José and Lisa. Fill in the times.

... I wake up around [1] ...., leave my flat around [2] ...., arrive at work [3] .... later ... my day normally ends around [4] ...., [5] ...., [6] ....

A normal day for me will be from [7] .... to [8] ....

I come to work at [9] .... and finish about [10] ....

⌐O

26

Second view

Are these statements true or false?

1 Once at work, Kerstin doesn't often move out of the Volvo building.
2 José doesn't take breaks.
3 Lisa always works the same hours. ⚷

Language work

Prepositions of time

Complete these sentences with a word from the box.

around in at till from

1 I wake up .... seven o'clock.
2 I come to work .... eight o'clock.
3 A normal day will be .... 8 o'clock .... half past seven ....
   the evening.

Can you remember who said these things: Kerstin, Lisa or José? ⚷

Practice

Write a paragraph about your own routine.

Remembering key vocabulary

**When you have corrected your work and looked at the tapescript, note six words
that are important to you in the space provided.**

nouns	verbs	expressions

Revise these words later by watching the sequence again and ✓ ticking the words
as you hear them. Try to remember the words in their context.

Part 3 Travel (06:15)

3.1 Kerstin Malmgren's travel plans (06:21)

Preview

Kerstin works in the public relations (PR) department of Volvo. It is her responsibility to promote the good name of Volvo.

Which of the following do you think are PR activities? 🔑

1 Holding information days for final year students at university.
2 Taking important customers out to lunch.
3 Giving interviews to journalists.
4 Sponsoring sporting events.
5 Doing market research.

What type of PR activities does your company or a company you know do?

First view

Circle the places Kerstin is going to and then number them in the order she will visit them. 🔑

Second view

Why is she visiting these places?

1 In Monte Carlo we have a .... and a test driving activity for ....

2 In Poland I'm going to a national final of a big activity called '..................... .... ' .

3 Austria is actually the .... of that activity. 🔑

Language work

Listening for language. Fill in the blanks in the first part of what Kerstin says.

I do [1] .... a lot, and as a matter of fact the coming weeks [2] ....
[3] .... to Monte Carlo next week, and a couple of weeks later I'm going
[4] .... Poland, and the week [5] .... [6] .... to Austria ... In
Poland [7] .... [8] .... to a national final of a big activity called
'Volvo European Safe Driver' ... 🔑

Grammar point

The present continuous tense
The present continuous can be used to describe an action going on at the present or to talk about future plans.

Find examples in the text on the previous page.   ⚷

Practice

Look at your diary and your appointments. Write a paragraph about your plans for the week saying where you are going and if possible why.

....
....
....   ⚷

3.2   The Monte Carlo seminar schedule (07:10)

Preview

Vocabulary work: match the words to the definitions.

1 to book   A to go on a plane which doesn't stop before its
2 to end   final destination
3 a direct flight   B to reserve a place
4 to pick someone up   C to collect, to go and get someone
                                        D to finish   ⚷

First view

Listen to Kerstin Malmgren talk about the schedule.

1 What day is Kerstin leaving: Saturday, Sunday or Monday?
2 How long does the seminar last: one, two or three days?
3 Who is the seminar for: mechanics, dealers or journalists?   ⚷

Second view

Complete the timetable for the journalists in Monte Carlo.

Volvo 850 series seminar
Monday
Arrive at [1] ....; picked up from airport
Start of seminar: [2] .... o'clock
In the evening: cocktails and [3] ....
Tuesday
In the morning: new [4] .... and [5] .... driving activity
Programme ends at [6] ....

Part 4 Likes and dislikes (08:13)

Preview

Check the meaning of the following words in a bilingual dictionary:

environment
personnel
atmosphere
maintenance
to weld

What do you like and dislike about your job or the job you are training for? Think about these things:

travel   variety
long hours   meetings
responsibility   your colleagues
stress   your office space

First view

Match the people to their statements about their jobs.

1 Martin
2 Birgitta
3 Kerstin
4 José

A *I don't like long meetings.*

B *I do a lot of different things.*

C *I have the chance to travel.*

D *I don't like people saying no to my ideas.*

E *The car industry is very interesting.*

Second view

Now watch again and complete the sentences.

Martin: One reason he likes his job is because it is *h*.................... *t*....................

Birgitta: She does four things;
  – *w*..........................
  – *m*..........................
  – looks after *p*..........................
  – goes to *m*..........................

Kerstin: She likes working for an *i*.......................... company.

José: He dislikes it when people say his ideas are *i*..........................

30

Language work

Notice the way the speakers talk about their likes and dislikes:

I like / dislike the job *because* it's …
I love work*ing* for an international company.

It is also possible to say:

I *enjoy* work*ing* …

Write a paragraph based on the following information. Alternatively, write about your own job.

John Roussel is an American who works as branch manager for his company in Paris.

Likes	Dislikes
Paris is a wonderful city.	He has to travel a lot and only has the weekends with his family.
He has a pleasant office in the middle of town.	He has to attend long meetings in French.
He is his own boss and he has the opportunity to do things he could never do in the States.	It takes a long time to get things done – there are so many forms to fill in.
The food is great.	long traffic jams

John loves living in Paris but …

Remembering key vocabulary

When you have corrected your work and looked at the tapescript for Parts 3 and 4, note words that are important to you in the space provided.

nouns	verbs	expressions

Revise these words later by watching the sequence again and ✓ ticking the words as you hear them. Try to remember the words in their context.

Part 5 Stress (09:44)

5.1 Dealing with stress (09:57)

Preview

Do you have a stressful job?

How do you deal with stress at work?

Which of the following do you think are good ways of dealing with stress?

smoking   exercise   planning your time   working less hours
having a short sleep after lunch   delegating work to others
taking work home   forgetting about work when you are at home
reading the newspaper   setting priorities   talking with colleagues
taking regular holidays   concentrating

Viewing task

Listen to what Kerstin and José say about managing stress. Tick (✓) those methods given above which they use.   🔑

5.2 Leisure activities (11:07)

Preview

Match the picture with the sport.   🔑

A swimming   E badminton
B weight lifting   F table tennis
C aerobics   G squash
D bowling

What sports do you do? Or like to watch?
Make a list.

Viewing task

Tick the Volvo facilities you see and the ones Lisa Nyberg mentions:

	Facilities you see	Facilities Lisa mentions
aerobics	☐	☐
badminton	☐	☐
bowling	☐	☐
squash	☐	☐
swimming	☐	☐
table tennis	☐	☐
tennis	☐	☐
weight lifting	☐	☐

🔑

Part 6 Working atmosphere and company culture (12:00)

Preview

Company culture
When we talk about a *company culture* we mean the attitude the company takes to its customers and employees.

Thinking point: which words would you use to describe your own (or a company you know) company culture?

First view

You are going to hear Kerstin Malmgren talking about Volvo company culture. What do you think she will say? What adjectives do you think she will use?

Now listen and see if you were right.

Second view

Listen again and fill in the gaps. 🔑─○

> I think Volvo has a very ¹ .... ² .... I mean you, I think you give people chances to
> ³ .... , to ⁴ .... , to be a part of
> ⁵ .... and feeling that they ⁶ ....

Remembering key vocabulary

When you have corrected your work and looked at the tapescript for Parts 5 and 6, note about six words or expressions that are important to you in the space provided.

verbs	sports	ways of dealing with stress	describing company culture

Revise these words later by watching the sequence again and ✔ ticking the words as you hear them. Try to remember the words in their context.

3 At the London Boat Show

Introduction

In this sequence we see people from two boat building companies describing and selling their product range. We visit one of the two manufacturers and then go to the London Boat Show.

The sequence lasts 11 minutes and is organised like this:

Part 1 About Fairline Boats (00:00)

1.1 The product range (00:21)

Preview

A twenty eight **footer** is a boat which
    measures 28 feet. (one foot = 0.348 metres)
A **cruiser** is a large motor boat.
A **product range** (or range of products)
    is a group of similar products with
    some differences and usually a
    different price.

First view

Listen to Guy Norrish, Sales and Marketing Director of Fairline Boats, and answer these questions. 🔑○

1 How many models are there in the range?
11, 13 or 30.
2 How much is the cheapest boat?
£15,000, £50,000 or £500,000.

Second view

Watch again and fill in the gaps. 🔑○

The range starts at [1] .... and for that you can have a [2] .... which will sleep [3] ....

At the other end of the range is the [4] .... foot squadron which sells for [5] .... pounds and sleeps up to [6] ....

Language work

Write a description of this product range. 🔑○

The Pen Collection

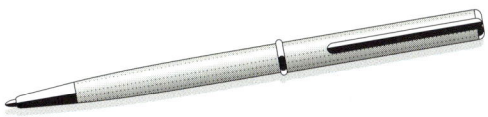

This beautiful solid silver pen has an engraved pattern on it. It is ideal for a very special present.
Price: £150

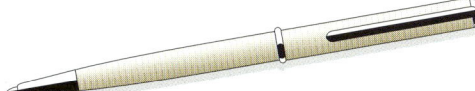

This lovely pen is gold plated (23 carat) and has a soft engraved pattern on it.
Price: £100

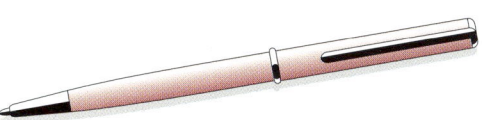

This pen comes in four bright colours and has a lacquer finish.
Price: £45

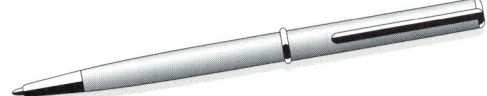

This smart pen is made in solid steel with a gold plated trim.
Price: £25

Use the following expressions:

The range starts at ...   At the other end of the range you go up to ...
In between ...

Grammar reminder

One syllable adjectives form their comparative and superlative with *-er* and *-est*: *small, smaller, smallest*. **Two** and **three syllable** adjectives form their comparatives and superlatives with *more* and *most*: *more interesting, most interesting*.

Some two syllable adjectives can also use *-er* and *-est*: *happy, happier, happiest*

1.2 The size of the company (00:53)

Preview

Check the meaning of these *departments* and *jobs* in your dictionary.

department	job
accounts	an accountant
sales	a salesperson
purchasing	a purchaser
design	a designer
	a carpenter
	an electrician
	an engineer

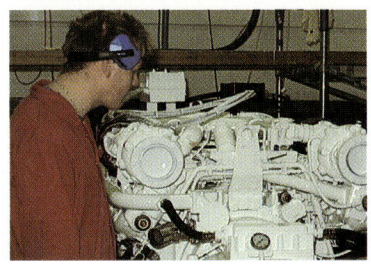

Which of the jobs are in manufacturing? 🔑

Vocabulary note : *a skilled worker*
   is a worker who has been
   trained to do his job.
An electrician is a *skilled* worker.

First view

Listen to Guy Norrish talking.

1 Approximately how many employees are there in total at Fairline?
   400, 460 or 500.
2 True or false? Most employees work in the administration.   🔑

Second view

Watch again.

1 What kind of people work in manufacturing? Find the adjective he uses.
   "all .... people"
2 Guy Norrish gives three examples of manufacturing jobs. What are they?   🔑

1.3 The main markets (01:36)

Viewing task

**Listen to Guy Norrish describing the market. Which chart correctly describes
Fairline's export markets?** 🔑

1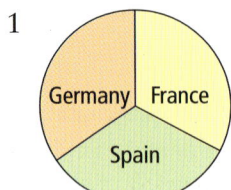

2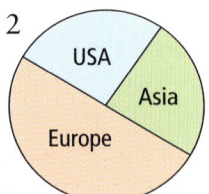

3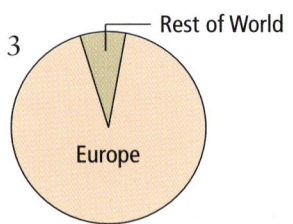

1.4 The importance of boat shows (02:02)

Preview

Important vocabulary in this part.

chief retailing activities = the most important ways of selling a product
a stand in an exhibition = the place where the product is displayed

Talking about numbers

go up to

go over/exceed

First view

Listen to Guy Norrish and tick the boat shows he mentions:

☐ Düsseldorf   ☐ Genoa   ☐ Miami
☐ Paris   ☐ Tokyo   ☐ Southampton
☐ Barcelona   ☐ Singapore   ☐ London

Second view

**Listen again to Guy Norrish. Are these statements true or false?
Correct the sentences if they are false.**

1 A Düsseldorf can attract up to 4,000,000 visitors.
   B The show at Genoa is an indoor show.
   C Southampton Boat Show is in September on the water.
   D The London Boat Show is in February.
   E The stand at the London Boat Show will be 1100 square metres.
   F The cost of the stand will be more than £250,000.
2 What's special for them about this year's show?

Remembering key vocabulary

When you have corrected your work and looked at the tapescript for Part 1, note about six words or expressions that are important to you in the space provided.

jobs	verbs	expressions

Revise these words later by watching the sequence again and ✓ ticking the words
as you hear them. Try to remember the words in their context.

Part 2 At the show (03:29)

Preview

Check the following words in your dictionary. Then watch the introduction to this part (03:29 to 04:21).
Do you see any of these things?

an exhibit   a motor boat
a stand   advertising
a range of products sales people

Vocabulary point: **shop window** is a place where products can be displayed.

2.1 The size of the London Boat Show (04:21)

Viewing task

Listen to Denzil Davies, Marketing Director of the London Boat Show, and answer these questions.

1 True or false? The show is only for the UK marine industry.
2 How many companies are at this year's show? 600, 615 or 650.   ⟋⚬

2.2 Finding out about Hunter Boats (04:45)

Hunter Horizon 21   Hunter Horizon 23   Hunter Ranger 265   Hunter Horizon 272   Hunter Horizon 30   Hunter Channel 32

First view

Listen to Andy Cunningham, a Hunter Boats salesman, talk about their boats. Tick (✓) the things Andy Cunningham speaks about.   ⟋⚬

the number of people that can go in the boat   ☐
the materials it is made of   ☐
the motor   ☐
the range of boats   ☐
the price   ☐

Second view

Listen again.

1 How many boats are there in the range? ....
2 How much is the least expensive? £..............
3 How much is the most expensive? £..............

2.3 Showing a customer the Hunter 265

Preview

Check the meaning of: **accommodation,
brand new** and **VAT** in your dictionary.

**Watch the first part of the sequence
without sound.
What do you think the people are saying?**

Now watch with sound. Were you right?

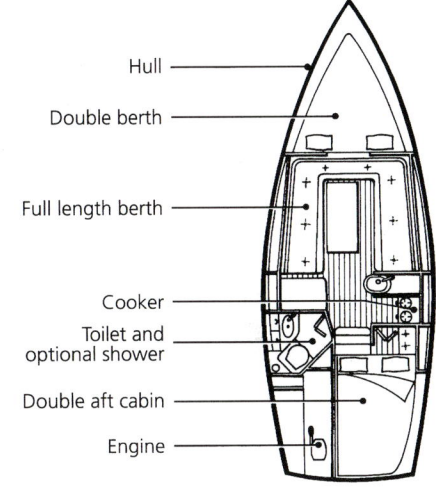

First view

**Watch Andy Cunningham showing the boat to a customer and answer these
questions.**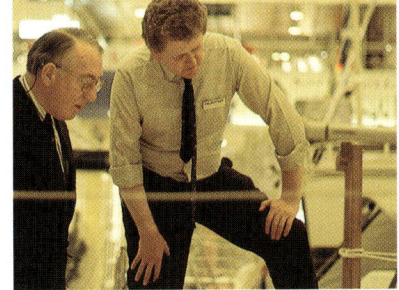

1 Tick (✓) the things the customer is interested in.
   accommodation for his family   ☐
   the speed of the boat   ☐
   the colour and the exterior of the boat ☐
   the price of the boat   ☐

2 Tick (✓) the things Andy talks about.
   sleeping arrangements   ☐
   cooking facilities   ☐
   speed   ☐
   size   ☐
   price   ☐
   fuel consumption   ☐

Second view

Watch this part again.

1 Has the boat been on the market for some time?
2 How much does the boat cost? £32,900, £31,900 or £30,900.
3 Does the price include VAT and the engine?

Language work

Fill in the gaps in the following dialogue.
Then listen and correct your answers.

Andy:
> Yes, [1] .... is our brand
> [2] .... Ranger 265 ... It's our
> [3] .... boat. It's a
> [4] .... new hull ... and it's got
> lots of [5] .... for the family.

Andy:
> Well, down below we [6] .... a double aft cabin
> to the stern. We have two full length berths in the
> [7] .... and then you've got room for
> [8] .... [9] .... to sleep at the front.

2.4 Showing a customer the Squadron 62 (07:03)

Preview

Important vocabulary in this part.

knots: 30 knots = 50 kilometers per hour
slightly = a little
easy to handle = easy to control
standard = usual, normal for this model
ready to go = prepared
steer = to control the direction of

First view

Listen to Guy Norrish showing two people the boat.

Tick (✓) the things they talk about.

☐ size
☐ colour
☐ speed
☐ the exterior of the boat
☐ sleeping space
☐ washing facilities

- Do you think the 265 is a good boat
  for this couple?

Second view

Watch this part again and correct the false statements.

1 The couple want a smaller boat than the one they've got now.
2 There is a 1000 horsepower Dutch engine on the Squadron 62.
3 The power steering and the hydraulic engine are extra.
4 The boat can sleep up to 8 people. 🔑

Language work

Look at the table showing details of the Fairline Squadron 62 and the Hunter Ranger 265. Then complete the sentences. 🔑

	Hunter Ranger 265	Fairline Squadron 62
Price	£32,900	£800,000
Length	26 feet	62 feet
Sleeping Accommodation	sleeps 6	sleeps 10
Engines	one inboard engine	two 1,000 horsepower engines

1 At £800,000 the 62 is .... the 265.
2 At 26 feet the 265 is .... the 62.
3 .... people can sleep on the 62 .... on the 265.
4 With two 1,000 horsepower engines the 62 is .... the 265.

Part 3   A successful show? (09:20)

Preview

Thinking point: what makes a show successful?

Vocabulary point: unit = a product or item

First view

Listen to Peter Poland, Marketing Director of Hunter Boats, and Guy Norrish of Fairline Boats.

1 Did Peter Poland have a good day at the show?

....

2 What does he spend a lot of time doing?

....

3 How does Guy Norrish describe the show?

....

4 How does this year compare with last year?

.... 🔑

Second view

Listen again to Peter Poland.

1 How many boats did Hunter sell?

....

Listen again to Guy Norrish.

2 How many boats did Fairline sell?

....

3 What was the total value of the Fairline sales?

£..........

Language work

Read the tapescript below and fill in the verbs.

Peter Poland

> *Today we* [1] .... *a very good day. We* [2] .... *a couple of sales, one to a chap who had* [3] .... *all the way from Germany, who* [4] .... *one of our 30 footers ... We have another man who* [5] .... *back and* [6] .... *an order on one of those ...*

Guy Norrish

> *It* [7] .... *an excellent show, probably the best one we've had for a number of years. We* [8] .... *over twenty units ...*

Now watch again and check your answers.

Remembering key vocabulary

When you have corrected your work and looked at the tapescript for part 2 and 3, note about six words or expressions related to *product presentation* or *sales* in the space provided.

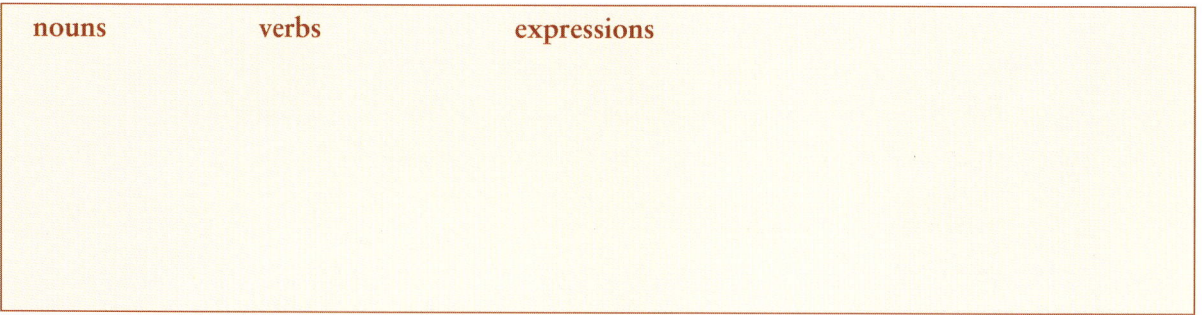

nouns	verbs	expressions

Revise these words later by watching the sequence again and ✔ ticking the words as you hear them. Try to remember the words in their context.

42

4 A business trip to Kuala Lumpur

Introduction

This sequence is about a business trip to Kuala Lumpur, the capital city of Malaysia, made by Deborah Wildridge, a British manager. She is part of a British *trade delegation* (a group of business people travelling together to do business). You see her at a hotel reception desk and on a visit to a factory. You also learn about Kuala Lumpur, in particular its spectacular economic growth.

The sequence lasts 12 minutes and is organised like this:

Part 1   **Booking a flight**
Part 2   **Things to do in Kuala Lumpur**
Part 3   **Deborah Wildridge's visit**
         3.1 Haldo Developments – its products and markets
         3.2 The value of the trade mission
         3.3 Visiting a company
Part 4   **Malaysia – a changing country**
         4.1 How Kuala Lumpur has changed
         4.2 Recent growth
         4.3 The future

Part 1   Booking a flight (00:00)

Preview

Travel vocabulary: check you know the meaning of these words. Use your dictionary.

Can you add any other words about travel?

First view

You are going to hear Christina at Malaysia Airlines in London giving information on the phone about flights. She talks about these things: number them in the order she talks about them.

☐ price of flights   ☐ conditions of ticket
☐ arrival time of flight   ☐ baggage allowance
☐ departure time of flight   ☐ check-in time

Second view

Complete the notes the caller made when listening to Christina.

Flight tonight at 1
Leaves from 2   Terminal 3
Check-in time 4
Fare £. 5
Baggage allowance .... kgs 6

Language work

Turn to the tapescript of the call on page 68 and write down what you think the caller said.

Extending key vocabulary

Complete the following table of words related to travel. Use your dictionary. Check your answers in the key.

Noun	Verb
a flight	....
....	to arrive
....	to depart
cancellation	....
a booking	....

Part 2

Things to do in Kuala Lumpur (01:13)

Viewing task

You are going to hear a Malaysian
taxi driver telling a passenger in his car
about things you can do in Kuala Lumpur. 🔑

Tick the things you see:

☐ people eating out
☐ a handicraft centre
☐ people lying on a beach
☐ the railway station and the National Mosque
☐ Chinatown
☐ people shopping in one of the shopping centres
☐ the National Museum

The taxi driver's English is not easy to
understand. Use the pictures to help you.

Part 3   **Deborah Wildridge's visit**

3.1   Haldo Developments – its products and markets (04:59)

Preview

Important vocabulary for this part.

a bollard =
in a nutshell = to say something in a few words
local authority = local government
contractor = company that supplies materials or workers
end user = person who uses/buys a product
booming = growing rapidly

First view

Listen to part of an interview with Deborah
Wildridge and answer these two questions. 🔑

1 What kind of products does she sell?
2 In which part of the world does she
   sell her products?

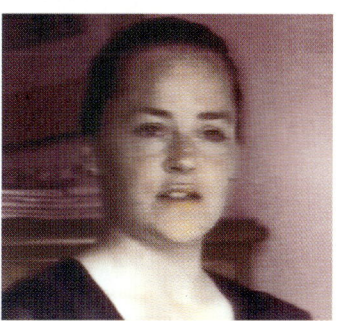

Second view

Listen to Deborah Wildridge again and complete these sentences.

1 Deborah Wildridge is the M........................ D........................ of Haldo
   Developments Ltd.
2 The technical term for bollards is street f........................ .
3 We sell to l........................ a........................ ... sometimes to p........................
   u........................ c........................ and sometimes to c........................ .   🔑

3.2 The value of the trade mission (05:40)

Preview

Important vocabulary for this part. Check with your dictionary if you need to.

trade reception = a party organised to allow foreign business people to meet
   business people in the country they are visiting
trade delegation/mission = group of people travelling together to do business
to have a good feel for = to understand well
beneficial = positive
local contacts = people living in the country you want to do business in who can
   help you and give you information
to get to know someone = to spend time with someone so that you become familiar
   with them

First view

**Listen to Eric Mattey and Deborah Wildridge speaking about trade missions. (Eric
Mattey is a British diplomat.) Are these sentences true or false?**

1 Eric Mattey says that the trade reception is for British people to meet only
   Malaysians.
2 Deborah Wildridge says that trade missions are not very useful.
3 Eric Mattey says that doing business in Asia is very different from doing
   business in the USA.
4 It takes time to do business in Asia.   🔑

Second view

Listen again and answer these questions.

1 Why does Eric Mattey say it's good to meet British people living in Malaysia?
2 Deborah Wildridge describes other members of the trade mission as
  e........................ and very g........................ in sharing their knowledge …
3 Why does Deborah Wildridge say it takes time to do business in South East
  Asia?

Language work

**Mark the word stress in the following words from the interview. The first one has
been done for you.**

reception   generous
purpose   beneficial
delegation   experienced
contacts (*the noun*)   knowledge
business

3.3 Visiting a company (06:58)

Preview

**In this part Deborah Wildridge visits a factory. Before you watch, read this
paragraph about the company Roadtech. Use your dictionary to help you if
necessary.**

Roadtech is a Malaysian company which makes road traffic signs and other road
construction equipment, like the paint used for marking roads. Deborah Wildridge visits
them because they may become distributors of Haldo Developments' products in Malaysia.

**Now watch from 06:58 to 07:40.
What do you think they are saying?
Note down your ideas.**

**Now listen. Did you hear any of
the words you noted?**

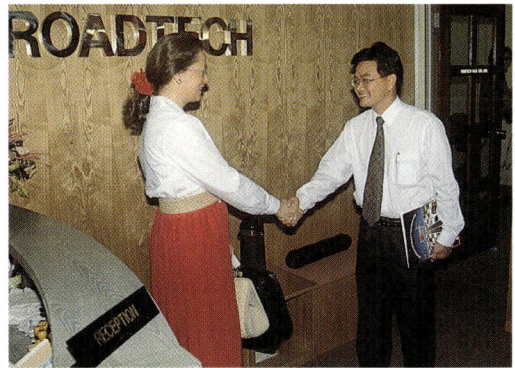

First view

Watch Deborah Wildridge visiting Roadtech and answer these questions.

1 Is it her first visit to Roadtech?
2 Do you think the people at Roadtech were helpful and friendly?
3 Which parts of the company do we see her in?

Second view

Watch again and complete the sentences.

I'm from Haldo Developments. [1] ....
[2] .... [3] .... [4] ....
with Mr Chua.

Deborah? [5] .... to Malaysia.

[6] .... [7] .... show you.

It's been [8] .... [9] .... and I'll
[10] .... [11] .... [12] .... when I
[13] .... [14] .... to England.

Language work

Look at these sentences from the visit. One is correct and one has an error of politeness or grammar. Decide which of the two is correct.

1 A *Hi, I'm Debbie!*   B *Good morning, I'm Deborah Wildridge.*

2 A *Would you mind to take a seat?*   B *Can you take a seat?*

3 A *Deborah wants to see you.*   B *Deborah is here to see you.*

4 A *Take my card.*   B *This is my card.*

5 A *Thanks a lot.*   B *Well, thank you very much indeed.*

6 A *Be careful.*   B *Take care.*

Practice 1

Complete Deborah Wildridge's notes on her visit to Roadtech.

Tuesday 1 March   Visit to [1] ....

I visited Roadtech this [2] .... and met Mr Chua. He
showed me round their [3] .... where they make
[4] .... I think they may be a useful [5] ....
for the future. They could [6] .... our street furniture
in Malaysia.

* Don't forget to write a [7] .... of thanks for the visit!

Practice 2

Write a letter of thanks to Mr Chua from Deborah Wildridge.

Remembering key vocabulary

When you have corrected your work and looked at the tapescript for Part 3, note about six words or expressions which are important for you. Look especially at 3.2 and at language to use with visitors.

nouns	verbs	expressions

Revise these words later by watching the sequence again and ✓ ticking the words as you hear them. Try to remember the words in their context.

Part 4 Malaysia – a changing country (08:49)

4.1 How Kuala Lumpur has changed (09:04)

Preview

Important vocabulary in this part.

skyline = shape of buildings against the sky
high rise = tall buildings

First view

Listen to Yoong Kim Yeng, a manager
at the Kuala Lumpur Stock Exchange, and
to Deborah Wildridge. 🔑

Has Kuala Lumpur changed a little or a lot?

Second view

Listen again and complete the text.

YOONG KIM YENG: Kuala Lumpur is very different from what it [1] .... ten
years [2] .... Nowadays we [3] .... got many modern buildings,
high rises and many modern facilities and amenities.

DEBORAH WILDRIDGE: I love to come back to KL. The second time I [4] .... it
felt like coming home to some extent because I'm more familiar with the road
system, where the buildings are. The skyline [5] .... changed completely in
a year [6] .... I last [7] .... but I find it a very comfortable city to
move around in, it's very easy. The food [8] .... delicious and I really
[9] .... at home this time. 🔑

Language work

Grammar point

Notice how the present perfect tense is used to describe change when you can see
the consequences of that change in the present: *The skyline has changed
completely.*

Make sentences about these situations.

1 inflation in 1995: 3.5% / inflation today 4.6%
2 women in government 1995: 4 / women in government today: 6
3 interest rates 1995: 6.5% / today 5.6% 🔑

Make a sentence about how your life, country or company has changed.

4.2 Recent growth (09:53)

First view

**Listen to Yoong Kim Yeng and Eric Mattey.
Answer this question.** 🔑

Yoong Kim Yeng and Eric Mattey both talk
about the same thing. What is it?

Second view

Listen again and write in the numbers.

YOONG KIM YENG: In terms of value of turnover, in [1] .... we have a total of
[2] .... billion ringgit. (In) 1993 it is 387.3 billion ringgit – an increase of
[3] .... The Kuala Lumpur Stock Exchange has grown from a small stock
exchange to the largest stock exchange in South-East Asia.

ERIC MATTEY: The future for Malaysia is actually very exciting because the country
has now been growing, the economy has been growing at about [4] .... per
cent for the last [5] .... years. 🔑

4.3 The future (10:49)

Preview

Important vocabulary in this part.

low tech activity = work which is **not** technically sophisticated
high tech (technological) activity = work which **is** technically sophisticated
shortage of labour = not enough workers

First view

Listen to Yoong Kim Yeng and Eric Mattey, and answer these questions.

1 What does Yoong Kim Yeng hope will **not** happen?
2 Why does Kuala Lumpur need to move to more high tech activities? 🔑

Second view

Listen again to what Eric Mattey says and fill in the gaps. The first letter of the missing word is given to you.

Eric Mattey:

I [1] s..................... the benefit to the individual is that they will have a
[2] m.................... [3] b.................... [4] s.................... [5] o.................... [6] l.................... .
The changes in the country: I think we will see a move from [7] l....................
t.................... m.................... activity to a much [8] h.................... technological type
of business which I think is [9] n.................... in Malaysia anyway because they have
a [10] s.................... of labour.   ⌐O

Language work

Grammar point

Notice how Yoong Kim Yeng and Eric Mattey use **will** to talk about how they see the future:

*I certainly hope that our people **will** not lose our cultural heritage.*
*I think we **will** see a move from low tech activity …*

Answer key with tapescripts

Welcome to Arthur D Little

Part 1 Registering at reception

First view

1 True;   2 No, it's at 9.15;   3 True

Second view

1 Probably not; she calls him "sir" which is not usually used by people who know each other.
2 Yes, she is. She asks how he is.
3 She asks him to register on a card.

Videoscript

THALIA SKOULOS: Good morning, sir.
TODD RHODES: Good morning. My name's Todd Rhodes. I'm here to see Tony Martrom.
THALIA SKOULOS: Very well. Would you kindly register on that blue card, if you would? And let's give you a badge. Here you are.
TODD RHODES: Thank you.
THALIA SKOULOS: And how are you this morning?
TODD RHODES: Very good, thank you.
THALIA SKOULOS: Good, good. And your appointment is at 9.15?
TODD RHODES: Yes.
THALIA SKOULOS: Very well. (*on the phone*) Oh, good morning Tony. This is Thalia at the desk. I have Mr Rhodes here for you. Thank you. (*to Todd Rhodes*) He'll be with you shortly.
TODD RHODES: Thank you very much.

Language work

1 My name's Todd Rhodes. I'm here to see Tony Martrom.
2 Would you kindly register on that blue card?
3 And let's give you a badge.
4 This is Thalia at the desk.
5 He'll be with you shortly.

Part 2 An overview of the business

2.1 The main business areas

Preview

1 B;   2 A;   3 C;   4 E;   5 D

First view

ADL is in **three** business areas.

Second view

1 Technology;   2 Product;   3 Consultants;   4 Safety;   5 Management;   6 Chinese

Videoscript

RANGANATH NAYAK: We're in three businesses: the first one of them is a business in which we develop new products and new technology for clients. It's basically R&D and there are two groups at Arthur D Little that do that kind of work: one is called the Technology and Product Development Directorate, which is based in Cambridge, Massachusetts, which I believe has roughly two hundred and fifty people in it, and then there's another group called Cambridge Consultants Limited, or CCL, which is in Cambridge, England, which has about two hundred people in it.

The second piece of our business is Environmental, Health and Safety Consulting and that's again a worldwide business.

And the third piece is what we call Management Consulting, in which we work with managers on the softer, more abstract problems, not actually doing R&D or solving environmental problems but solving problems of strategy or acquisition of new businesses, or how to go global, how to enter into the Chinese market, etcetera. What our customers need to know is we're in three businesses.

Language work

Further practice

Example answer

```
The name of the company is New Jersey Books. It is based in New York
but has branches in fourteen countries. It has over two thousand
employees. Its annual turnover is roughly five hundred million
dollars. New Jersey Books is in the publishing business; it works in
three areas: magazines and books, music and videos. Magazines and
books are sold worldwide, their videos are sold in Europe and the USA.
Their music is only sold in Europe.
```

2.2 The size of the business

Preview

1 turnover
3 .52 is roughly a half / point 5.
   1,505 is approximately / roughly one thousand five hundred.
   2,001 is just over two thousand.

First view

1 about 2,600 employees
2 30 to 40
3 about 1,500 consultants
4 turnover is about $300 million

Second view

1 About 50% of employees work in the USA.
2 6 (half a dozen) offices are in the USA.
3 No, he only mentions 9.

Videoscript

RANGANATH NAYAK: Altogether we have about 2,600 employees, and they're roughly half in the United States and half outside of the United States. We have offices now in about thirty to forty cities – I couldn't remember all of them, but they include place London, Paris, Berlin, Frankfurt, Moscow, Hong Kong, Taipei, Sydney, Tokyo, which gives you a sample and including Latin America as well, and then half a dozen offices here in North America.

Of the 2,600 total staff, I would estimate that about 1,500 are consultants. The turnover of the company fluctuates a bit because of the way the exchange rates go but now it's roughly around $300 million per year.

Language work

1 consultancy; 2 three; 3 Research; 4 Health; 5 Management; 6 world;
7 turnover; 8 headquarters

Part 3 Meet some people in the company

Preview

1 D; 2 C; 3 B; 4 E; 5 F; 6 A

First view

1 G; 2 B; 3 A; 4 F; 5 D; 6 C; 7 E; 8 H

Second view

1 Ranganath Nayak; 2 Carl Johnson; 3 Mary Janaitis; 4 Ranganath Nayak

Videoscript

RANA GUPTA: My name is Rana Gupta. I'm a consultant in the Environmental Business and Strategy practice area.
RAN: I'm Ranganath Nayak. People have trouble with my whole name so they usually call me Ran or Rarn, and I'm a Senior Vice President at Arthur D Little and a member of the management committee here.
DONNA DEDOMENICO: My name's Donna DeDomenico. I'm a secretary here in Environmental Management.
JOE BOTTARI: My name is Joe Bottari. I'm the Supervisor of the printing, photocopying, binding unit of the Arthur D Little Communication Services print shop.
MARY JANAITIS: My name is Mary Janaitis and I'm a Human Resources generalist, a manager here at Arthur D Little, and I do a wide range of things.
CARL JOHNSON: My name is Carl Johnson and currently I am the Traffic Manager for Arthur D Little Company in Cambridge and I'm involved in all aspects of moving of freight, mail, courier deliveries – inbound and outbound.
MELISSA RIGATTI: My name's Melissa Rigatti and my job is Laboratory Supervisor for the Marine Chemistry group.
CONNIE COPPINGER: My name is Constance Coppinger. My friends call me Connie, and I am a Support Staff Administrator here in the Environmental, Health and Safety Directorate.

Language work

1 con<u>sul</u>tant; 2 <u>ma</u>nagement; 3 <u>se</u>cretary; 4 <u>su</u>pervisor; 5 re<u>sou</u>rces;
6 de<u>li</u>veries; 7 la<u>bo</u>ratory; 8 environ<u>men</u>tal

Part 4 Behind the scenes

4.1 In the Copy Center

Preview

ADL's main product is **advice** to companies. This is often in the form of documents or reports.

First view

1 photocopying; 2 printing; 3 binding

Second view

reports; proposals; factsheets

Videoscript

JOE BOTTARI: This is the Copy Center of the Arthur D Little Communication Services Department and we do printing, photocopying and binding for most of the corporation here. Mainly reports and proposals that go to Arthur D Little clients around the world. This is what we call a fact sheet: this is done for our sections and it describes the type of work that the company does in a certain given area. It's a market …, these are marketing pieces basically.

4.2 On the phone

Preview

1 Say *Hello*, the name of your company and then your own name + *speaking*, for example *Hello, this is New Jersey Books, Paul speaking.*
2 *Could you hold the line. I'll put you through.*
3 *You're welcome* (if the person has said *thank you*). *Goodbye.*

First view

She takes a message.

Second view

E; C; D; B; A

Videoscript

DONNA DEDOMENICO: Environmental Management, Donna speaking. … I'm sorry he's not in the office right now. Could I have him call you back? … And can you spell that, please? … OK. OK. And your phone number there, please? … Very good. I'll have him call you back. … You're welcome. Bye bye.

Language work

Example dialogue

DONNA: Environmental Management, Donna speaking.
CALLER: Hello. Could I speak to John Fleming please?
DONNA: I'm sorry he's not in the office right now. Could I have him call you back?
CALLER: Yes, could you? My name's Gabriella Tomaszewski.
DONNA: And can you spell that please?
CALLER: T O M A S Z E W S K I.
DONNA: And your phone number there, please?
CALLER: 289 0706.
DONNA: Very good, I'll have him call you back.
CALLER: Thank you very much.
DONNA: You're welcome. Bye bye.

Part 5 The Technology and Product Development Directorate

5.1 Working with the food industry

First view

She is a *Vice* president not a *Senior* vice president and *Managing* Director.
Her specialty is food *ingredient* technology not food *preservatives*.
She has a PhD in *chemical* engineering not *biological* engineering.
She has worked in the *food* industry for 14 years.

Second view

1 This;   2 who;   3 group;   4 product

Videoscript

GAIL GREENWALD: My name is Gail Greenwald. I'm a Vice President and Managing Director of Technology Consulting here at ADL. My background is chemical engineering; I have a PhD in chemical engineering and have been working in the food industry for the last 14 years. My specialty is food ingredient technology. In the lab we do a lot of food product development, and we help clients either who are food companies themselves or who have, for example, ingredients that they'd like to sell to food companies.

This is Vanick Petrossian, who's one of our senior people in product development in the food group. Today we're working on a mixture of fruits which we're using as a base in a new product that we're working on. How's the papaya working? You haven't tried the papaya yet?

VANICK PETROSSIAN: We'll try that tomorrow. That's what I'm doing now. We'll try that for tomorrow.

GAIL GREENWALD: What's this?

VANICK PETROSSIAN: That's coconut.

GAIL GREENWALD: Oh …

Language work

Example answer

My name is Gabriella Tomaszewski. I'm a lawyer in a big company in Warsaw. I have a master's degree in international law and I specialise in company law.

5.2 Two examples of product development

First view

a pencil and a bicycle

Second view

1 It is made of plastic;   2 its weight

Videoscript

DAVID LEE: We are in energy, medical products, military and space, information communications technology, the chemical industry – those are the main practice areas.

The pencil's an old development but still quite lively in the market place. There's, I think 30% of the market is now these plastic pencils and so to know whether you've got one, you can bend it a little bit and if it bends, it's a plastic pencil.

And another example of a product of some interest to many people here was recently completed, was the development of a very lightweight bicycle frame for a European manufacturer of bicycles. That manufacturer, having to compete worldwide, was making steel framed bicycles and we helped them develop a carbon fibre epoxy-based frame that reduced the weight of the frame from four pounds to about two and a half pounds. It made the bike a lot more competitive and rugged.

Language work

-ical	-tion	-logy
che<u>mi</u>cal	infor<u>ma</u>tion	tech<u>no</u>logy
<u>me</u>dical	communi<u>ca</u>tion	bi<u>o</u>logy
<u>tech</u>nical	presen<u>ta</u>tion	

Rule: in most words ending with these suffixes, the stress is just *before* the suffix.

Part 6 The Environmental, Health and Safety Directorate

Preview

The owner of a landfill site needs to find a way to manage the land. He could have a problem with local government and people who live near the site and who are unhappy about living next to a site which is not beautiful and is possibly dangerous to their health.

First view

1 He helps with environmental, health and safety concerns.
2 He spends a long time travelling in the Far East.

Second view

1 life	5 health	9 doing
2 people	6 time	10 setting up
3 problems	7 abroad	11 systems
4 environmental	8 working	

Videoscript

ANTHONY HYDE: Most of my working life is spent helping clients solve problems with environmental, health or safety concerns. Today I'm at a landfill site, helping our client with some environmental problems.
   A lot of my time is spent abroad, a lot of the time in the Far East, working with clients doing safety auditing, setting up safety management systems, and that sort of thing. Other than that, we spend a lot of time writing reports, giving presentations and presenting papers at conferences.

Part 7 The Management Consultancy Directorate

7.1 The Management Consultancy's clients

Preview

Management consultants are usually called when there are problems. For example when two parts of the company don't work well together or when there are financial problems.

First view

B

Second view

Chemicals; energy; pharmaceuticals; banking; metals; automotive; aerospace

Videoscript

KARL LOOS: I believe at last count there were 15 priority industries that we offered management consulting services to; chemicals, energy, pharmaceuticals, automotive, information systems, aerospace, pulp and paper, metals, I could go on, banking.

7.2 How the Management Consultancy Directorate is organised

Preview

1 segment;   2 boundary

First view

There are four segments.

Second view

Map 3 which shows North America, Europe, Latin America and Asia Pacific

Videoscript

KARL LOOS: Management consulting in ADL is divided first along geographic boundaries: four geographic business segments – North America, Europe, Latin America and Asia Pacific. And each one of these operates as a semi-autonomous business, Management Consulting being one of the three major businesses at Arthur D Little.

Part 8 ADL – the perfect partner?

First view

False: very few do both environmental and technical consulting.

Second view

Example answer

The Vice President believes that ADL is in a unique position to help companies because it is able to work in the three areas of technical and product development, environmental health and safety and management consulting. Most other consulting companies only work in one of these areas.

Videoscript

RANGANATH NAYAK: We are one of the broadest consulting firms in the range of services that we provide. We have a number of companies that compete with us in management consulting but very few of them provide environmental or technology consulting. And similarly we have companies that compete with us in the environmental field but they don't do management consulting. We are one of the few firms that spans all three areas.

SEQUENCE 2 ## Working for Volvo Car Corporation

Introduction

Volvo is especially famous for building safe, reliable vehicles and for its concern for people and the environment.

In the introduction you see 1, 4, 5, 6, 8 and 10.

Part 1 Talking about your work

Preview

1 C; 2 D; 3 B; 4 A; 5 F; 6 E

First view

1 C; 2 A; 3 B; 4 E; 5 D

Second view

1 floor; 2 put together; 3 advice; 4 marketing; 5 Brussels; mid June

Videoscript

BIRGITTA HOPKINS: We produce the floor, the sides and roof on the actual car – just the shell of the car, nothing else. I am responsible for the shift. I see that we have sufficient personnel each day to carry out the duties in the factory.

CHRISTER WEISS: My responsibility is to put together engines so we can put them over to the chassis line.

LISA NYBERG: Can I have your arm please, the back of your arm? … I think most of the people come to see me 'cause they feel that something is wrong in their lives, they want to change something. And what I do is give them advice and support them.

JOSÉ: What do you think?

COLLEAGUE: I think it's good.

JOSÉ: Does it look better than all monochrome?

COLLEAGUE: Yeah, yeah.

JOSÉ: It seems to have a little more value, doesn't it?

COLLEAGUE: Yeah, yeah.

JOSÉ: Yeah?

JOSÉ L. DIAZ DE LA VEGA: In the, in the nineties design is now a marketing tool. It's really, it has become a marketing tool, so if it is used properly design is very close to the customer. The main goal for us is to produce the most desirable Volvos we can do in the future.

KERSTIN MALMGREN: Hi there.

INGRID ALM: So, what about your plans for next week?

KERSTIN MALMGREN: Yes, I'm just looking into that. I have to leave on the Saturday, actually, because we have meetings starting in the morning of Sunday and we also have to put in exhibition material …

KERSTIN MALMGREN: I work as a PR manager, for the time being in Europe, based in Brussels, but I will actually move back to Sweden in mid-June.

Language work

enough	sufficient
make	produce
the majority	most
at the moment	for the time being
assemble	put together
What's your opinion?	What do you think?
someone who buys	customer

Part 2 Routines

2.1 In the factory

Preview

shift: a group of workers who do a job for a period of time during the day or night (*Cambridge International Dictionary of English*)

First view

1 two;   2 two;   3 45 minutes;   4 25 days;
5 Because she gets Friday off and has a long weekend

Second view

Birgitta's working week

	number of days worked	start	finish
early shift	5	5.48	14.36
late shift	4	14.36	23.42

Christer's working week

	start	finish
day shift	6.30	–
night shift	16.00	–

Videoscript

BIRGITTA HOPKINS: I work two shifts. I work one early week and I work one late week. The difference between the two shifts is that we work early shift one week when we start early in the morning at 5.48 and finish at 14.36, and on the late shift we start at 14.36 and finish at 23.42. And on the early shift we work five days a week and on the late shift we work four days a week, which means that we have the Friday off, so we have a very nice long weekend there.

CHRISTER WEISS: The day shift starts 6.30 in the morning and the night shift starts about four o'clock in the afternoon. Coffee breaks – we have about two short coffee breaks and a 45 minutes lunchtime break as well.
BIRGITTA HOPKINS: We get 25 days' holiday a year.

2.2 *In the offices*

First view

1 seven;   2 eight;   3 twenty minutes;   4 six o'clock;   5 six-thirty;   6 seven;
7 eight o'clock;   8 half past seven;   9 eight o'clock;   10 five o'clock

Second view

1 True
2 True: he doesn't stop to take a break.
3 False: sometimes she works later than five.

Videoscript

KERSTIN MALMGREN: If I am in Brussels, I wake up around seven, leave my flat around eight, arrive at work twenty minutes later and, er, we are based a little bit outside the city centre so actually we don't move around a lot; we stay at the office, we eat in the same building, and normally my day ends around six, six-thirty, seven.
JOSÉ L. DIAZ DE LA VEGA: A normal day for me will be from eight o'clock to half past seven in the evening.
INTERVIEWER: And do you get any breaks?
JOSÉ L. DIAZ DE LA VEGA: The breaks are as we walk along.
LISA NYBERG: I come to work at eight o'clock in the morning and finish about five o'clock in the evening – could be later. Work five days a week and, well, that's it!

Language work

1 around, or, at (Kerstin);   2 at (Lisa);   3 from, till, in (José)

Practice

Example paragraph

I get up at a quarter to seven and have a coffee. Then I dress and watch the television news. At 8 am I leave the house and drive to work. I work from 8.30 to 6.30 except on Fridays when I try to leave the office at 6 o'clock.

Part 3 Travel

3.1 *Kerstin Malmgren's travel plans*

Preview

1 Holding information days could be PR but it is probably more important for recruiting graduates – the personnel department's responsibility.
2 This is both PR and commercial.
3 PR.
4 PR.
5 Commercial and marketing, not really PR.

First view

She will visit Monte Carlo, Poland and Austria (in that order).

Second view

1 In Monte Carlo we have a *seminar* and a test driving activity for *journalists*.
2 In Poland I'm going to a national final of a big activity called '*Volvo European Safe Driver*'.
3 Austria is actually the *European final* of that activity.

Videoscript

KERSTIN MALMGREN: I do travel a lot, and as a matter of fact the coming weeks I'm going to Monte Carlo next week, and a couple of weeks later I'm going to Poland, and the week after that to Austria. In Monte Carlo we have a seminar and a test driving activity for journalists – family magazines, life style magazines, etcetera. In Poland I'm going to a national final of a big activity called 'Volvo European Safe Driver', taking place in all European markets, and Austria is actually the European final of that activity.

Language work

1 travel;   2 I'm;   3 going;   4 to;   5 after;   6 that;   7 I'm;   8 going

Grammar point

An example of the present continuous to talk about future plans is *I'm going to Monte Carlo.*

Practice

Example answer

On Monday I'm going to Bristol for the day to participate in a seminar on training. From Tuesday to Thursday I'll be in the office but on Friday I won't be at work. I'm going to London for the weekend for a friend's wedding.

3.2 The Monte Carlo seminar schedule

Preview

1 B;   2 D;   3 A;   4 C

First view

1 Kerstin is leaving on Saturday.
2 The seminar lasts two days.
3 The seminar is for journalists.

Second view

1 noon;   2 three;   3 dinner;   4 presentation;   5 test;   6 two o'clock

Videoscript

KERSTIN MALMGREN: So, sometime during Saturday, preferably in the afternoon. Direct flight.
INGRID ALM: OK. But I mean direct flight is more important than, er, …
KERSTIN MALMGREN: The time, yes, I think so.
INGRID ALM: But if there is an early one, I'll book you on that one.
KERSTIN MALMGREN: Good. And when am I seeing the mechanic and the exhibition guy?
INGRID ALM: You are seeing them just before lunch, 11, 11.30.
KERSTIN MALMGREN: On Monday?
INGRID ALM: On Monday, yes.
KERSTIN MALMGREN: They arrive, the journalists arrive around noon Monday, will be picked up at the airport, and then the seminar starts in the afternoon at three o'clock. After that, we have a cocktail and a dinner for the journalists. In the morning the next day we have a new presentation and then a test driving activity. And the programme ends with a lunch at around two o'clock. And then they go back home.

Part 4 Likes and dislikes

First view

A Kerstin;   B Birgitta;   C Kerstin;   D José;   E Martin

Second view

Martin: he likes his job because it is high tech.

Birgitta: she does four things:
- weld
- maintenance
- looks after personnel
- goes to meetings

Kerstin: likes working for an international company.

José: doesn't like it when people say his ideas are impossible.

Videoscript

MARTIN RYBECK: First, I think to work in a car industry is tremendously interesting. It's high technology and also the environment with the people, I think it's a very good atmosphere in our company.

BIRGITTA HOPKINS: I like the job simply because it's very variable. I do maintenance and I weld and I look after personnel, I go to meetings, so it is very, very variable.

KERSTIN MALMGREN: I love working for an international company, that's number one. And you have the opportunity, I mean, really to travel around and see other parts of the world.
What I don't like is the long meetings we have sometimes.

JOSÉ L. DIAZ DE LA VEGA: When we present something from design to a group and they can tell, and they tell us it cannot be done, it is impossible or nobody will notice – that I dislike. I, I cannot accept obstacles before we have even started.

Language work

Example answer

John loves living in Paris but he dislikes the travelling he does for his job. He doesn't like being away from his family. He likes his office but he doesn't enjoy going to long French meetings. He enjoys his independence but dislikes the amount of paperwork there is. He loves eating good French food and drinking wine from France. However, he doesn't like driving when there are traffic problems.

Part 5 Stress

5.1 Dealing with stress

Viewing task

They talk about: exercise; planning your time and delegating.

Videoscript

KERSTIN MALMGREN: You can't do ten things at the same time so planning and concentrating is a good start. Delegating is another good thing to do. And then, especially for the people working here in Gothenburg, you have a lot of places for relaxation. I mean, you can go to the centre we have around here, the fitness centre, to do your workout or to swim or anything like that.

JOSÉ L. DIAZ DE LA VEGA: I like exercise, so when I am free I tend to exercise in different ways. Another way to do it, of course, is within: you tell yourself 'I am going to do this', sort of set priorities. And I think by setting these priorities it helps you to release some of this stress.

5.2 Leisure activities

Preview

aerobics	squash
table tennis	swimming
badminton	bowling
weight lifting	

Viewing task

You see	Lisa mentions
aerobics	swimming
badminton	weight lifting
bowling	aerobics
swimming	tennis
weight lifting	

Videoscript

LISA NYBERG: You have swimming facilities, weight lifting facilities, aerobic classes, bowling, tennis playing, things like that.

Part 6 Working atmosphere and company culture

Second view

1 open;   2 attitude;   3 influence;   4 react;   5 decisions;   6 belong

Videoscript

KERSTIN MALMGREN: I think Volvo has a very open attitude. I mean you, I think you give people chances to influence, to react, to be a part of decisions and feeling that they belong. We talked earlier about the Volvo spirit which was quite well known; I think it still exists.

SEQUENCE 3 At the London Boat Show

Part 1 About Fairline Boats

First view

1 13;   2 £50,000

Second view

1 £50,000;   2 28 footer;   3 four;   4 62;   5 three quarters of a million;   6 ten

Videoscript

GUY NORRISH: The range starts at just over £50,000, and for that you can have a 28 footer which will sleep four people – it's a fully equipped sea-going cruiser. And at the other end of the range you go right up to the 62 foot Squadron, which sells for about three quarters of a million pounds, can sleep up to ten people, and in between we have another 11 models – there are 13 altogether in the range.

Language work

Example answer

The range starts at £25 with the solid steel pen with the gold plated trim.
At the other end of the range you have a solid silver pen with an engraved design; it's the most expensive pen in the range at just over £150. In between there is a gold plated pen at £100 or a coloured lacquered pen at £45.

1.2 The size of the company

Preview

Manufacturing: a carpenter; an electrician; an engineer

First view

1 500 employees.
2 False, most employees work in manufacturing.

Second view

1 all *skilled* people
2 carpenters; engineers; electricians

Videoscript

GUY NORRISH: On this site we have all of the administration, so there's about 40 people involved in accounts, sales, purchasing, design. That leaves about 460 employed in manufacturing – all skilled people, chiefly carpenters, engineers, electricians and so forth.

1.3 The main markets

Viewing task

Chart 3

Videoscript

GUY NORRISH: 90% of our sales are within Europe and within that, although we sell a lot in the UK, a lot of that itself then goes abroad, and our main export markets are Germany, France, Italy, Spain.

1.4 The importance of boat shows

First view

He mentions all except Miami.

Second view

1 A False. Up to 400,000 visitors.   D False. It is in January.
   B False. It's outdoors.   E True.
   C True.   F False. More than £200,000.
2 It will be the largest stand at the show and their largest ever show.

Videoscript

GUY NORRISH: Our chief retailing activities take place at boat shows. There are up to 20 major ones which we attend. The big ones internationally are Düsseldorf, which can attract up to 400,000 visitors, Paris, Barcelona; Genoa is the largest of the outdoor shows. We also are at shows in Tokyo and Singapore and throughout the world really, but the biggest of all of them from our point of view are the two UK ones, one on the water at Southampton in September and the other major one is London at Earls Court in January. Our stand at London this year will be the largest one of any one, and the largest one we've ever had. It is, in terms of space, 1100 square metres; 13 boats will be exhibited on that. Altogether the costs for a stand that size probably exceed £200,000.

Part 2 At the show

2.1 The size of the London Boat Show

Viewing task

1 False. It is also a shop window for the international marine industry.
2 650.

Videoscript

DENZIL DAVIES: It's a shop window for the UK marine industry; this is also a shop window for the international marine industry. Although it's predominantly UK companies here, we do have a lot of international companies. This year we have 650, which is a very good number. We've filled all the spaces – no empty space.

2.2 Finding out about Hunter boats

First view

Andy Cunningham speaks about the *range of boats* and the *price*.

Second view

1 six;   2 £10,000;   3 £60,000

Videoscript

ANDY CUNNINGHAM: This is our new boat, the Hunter Ranger. It actually fits in very nicely with our boats; we now have a Hunter 23, the Ranger 265, and our Hunter Channel 32, which are exceedingly good sturdy family cruising boats. It actually complements our 21, our 27, and our 30, which are perhaps a little bit more sporty family cruising boats for those people who might want to do some club racing. … Well, our 21 works out at about £10,000 and we go right up to the Channel 32, which you can get for about £60,000.

2.3 Showing a customer the Hunter 265

First view

1 The customer is interested in:
   – accommodation for his family
   – the price of the boat
2 Andy Cunningham talks about:
   – sleeping arrangements
   – cooking facilities
   – size (indirectly : lots of accommodation, room)
   – price

Second view

1 No, it is brand new.
2 £32,900.
3 Yes, the price includes VAT and the engine.

Videoscript

ANDY CUNNINGHAM: Good morning.
CUSTOMER: Good morning. Is this the boat I saw featured on television?
ANDY CUNNINGHAM: Yes, this is our brand new Ranger 265 that everybody is raving about. It's our newest boat. It's a brand new hull, brand new deck and it's got lots of accommodation for the family.
CUSTOMER: Yes, that's what interests me really. I've got a family of three children, so it'll be my wife and three children that will be using it. Can you show me the boat?
ANDY CUNNINGHAM: Yes, certainly – step aboard.
CUSTOMER: Well, how many berths has it got?
ANDY CUNNINGHAM: Well, down below we have a double aft cabin to the stern. We have two full length berths in the middle and then you've got room for two adults to sleep right at the very front. … Well, here you can see the main living area. You've got the galley behind you. There's the cooker, the two burners and the grill, and of course behind you you have the toilet, and there is room in there for a shower if you wish.
CUSTOMER: That's very impressive. How much does this boat cost?
ANDY CUNNINGHAM: This boat is £32,900, including the VAT and the inboard engine.

Language work

1 this;   2 new;   3 newest;   4 brand;   5 room;   6 have;   7 middle;   8 two;
9 adults

2.4 Showing a customer over the Squadron 62

First view

They talk about:
- size
- speed
- sleeping space
- washing facilities

Second view

1 False. They want a larger boat.
2 False. It has a German engine.
3 False. They are standard to the boat.
4 True.

Videoscript

MAN: We've got a 51 foot Fairline and we want to go up to a slightly larger size, so we're here today to see what you can offer us.

GUY NORRISH: Right. This is our top-of-the-range flagship boat, 62 feet long, sleeps up to ten people. Well, let's have a look around, shall we?

MAN: And what sort of speed would you get out of this boat with the engines that you've got in it?

GUY NORRISH: The engines on this are a pair of 1,000 horsepower German engines, will take this boat along at about 31 knots.

WOMAN: How easy is it to handle with a minimum number of crew?

GUY NORRISH: This boat has power steering and hydraulic engine controls: separate gear and throttle controls – very easy to use. And that controls one of the two 1,000 horsepower engines. All this equipment is standard; you have a radar on here …

WOMAN: We like to entertain a lot. How many people does this boat sleep?

GUY NORRISH: There are different options to the layouts you can have, but most often we've fitted it with four cabins, and the largest of these is the one we're in now. It has its toilet just here and a separate shower on the other side. In comfort with those four cabins you can sleep eight people – they're all twins or doubles. If you want it to be more luxurious, we can in fact turn the port cabin …

MAN: What's the price of the basic boat?

GUY NORRISH: The boat as you see it with all the standard features here is round about £800,000.

MAN: And that gives us virtually everything we need, doesn't it?

GUY NORRISH: Ready to go, yes.

MAN: Right. What do you think?

WOMAN: It's lovely. A very nice boat indeed.

Language work

1 At £800,000 the 62 is more expensive than the 265.
2 At 26 feet the 265 is not as long as the 62.
3 More people can sleep on the 62 than on the 265.
4 With two 1,000 horsepower engines the 62 is faster than the 265.

Part 3 A successful show?

First view

1 Yes, a very good day.
2 He spends a lot of time talking to people.
3 He describes it as excellent.
4 They sold many more boats than they did last year.

Second view

1 Hunter sold a couple of boats and is in the middle of selling a third one.
2 Fairline sold over 20.
3 £5 million.

Videoscript

PETER POLAND: Today we had a very good day, in fact. We had a couple of sales, one to a chap who had come all the way from Germany, who bought one of our 30 footers, that's that one there. We had another man who came back and confirmed an order on one of those. We have a gentleman over there right now confirming an order on one of our 26's. It's a very exhausting pastime because you spend a lot of time talking to people, but it's an essential part of marketing a product on an international basis.

GUY NORRISH: It was an excellent show, probably the best one we've had for a number of years. We sold over twenty units, probably about five million pounds worth of boats, and we certainly sold far more boats this year than we did the same period last year.

Language work

1 had;   2 had;   3 come;   4 bought;   5 came;   6 confirmed;   7 was;   8 sold

SEQUENCE 4   A business trip to Kuala Lumpur

Part 1 Booking a flight

First view

4 price of flights	5 conditions of ticket
2 arrival time of flight	6 baggage allowance
1 departure time of flight	3 check-in time

Second view

1 10 o'clock;   2 Heathrow;   3 Terminal 3;   4 2 hours before departure;   5 £789;
6 20 kgs

Videoscript

CHRISTINA: Good morning, Malaysia Airlines, Christina speaking. Can I help you? … We do have a flight this evening. Departure time is at ten o'clock; arrival into Kuala Lumpur is at six-thirty the following evening. … That's from Heathrow, Terminal Three. You'd need to check in at least two hours before departure … The fare – would that be in Economy Class? … It's £789 based on a PEX fare, has seven days' minimum stay, three months' maximum and is subject to £50 change or cancellation fee. … That would be 20 kilos in Economy Class. … Can I take your surname? … And your initial?…

CHRISTINA: Good afternoon. Malaysia Airlines. Christina speaking. Can I help you?

CUSTOMER: Good afternoon. Do you have a flight to Kuala Lumpur today?

CHRISTINA: We do have a flight this evening. Departure time is at ten o'clock; arrival into Kuala Lumpur is at six-thirty the following evening.

CUSTOMER: Good. Which airport is that from and what time do I need to be there?

CHRISTINA: That's from Heathrow, Terminal Three. You'd need to check in at least two hours before departure.

CUSTOMER: How much is the ticket?

CHRISTINA: The fare – would that be in Economy Class?

CUSTOMER: Yes.

CHRISTINA: It's £789 based on a PEX fare, has seven days' minimum stay, three months' maximum and is subject to £50 change or cancellation fee.

CUSTOMER: Fine. And what's the baggage allowance?

CHRISTINA: That would be 20 kilos in Economy Class.

CUSTOMER: OK. I'd like to make a reservation.

CHRISTINA: Can I take your surname?

CUSTOMER: Yes, it's …

CHRISTINA: And your initial?

CUSTOMER: It's …

Language work

Extending key vocabulary

Noun	Verb
a flight	to fly
arrival	to arrive
departure	to depart
cancellation	to cancel
a booking	to book

Part 2 Things to do in Kuala Lumpur

Viewing task

We see: people eating out; a handicraft centre; the railway station and the National Mosque; Chinatown; people shopping in one of the shopping centres

Videoscript

TAXI DRIVER: In Kuala Lumpur there are many places to see. One of the places to see, first thing, is the Chinatown. That's where lots of foreigners go. Bright lights at night, fruit sellers, a lot of small things, clothes, watches.

(*Scenes in Chinatown*)

MAN: How much is this one?

SELLER: This one. This one you want – 110.

MAN: 110?

SELLER: Yeah.

MAN: The other one, the other one gave me 60.

WOMAN: Hi. Can you tell me how much this one is, please?

SELLER: This?

WOMAN: Yeah, how much?

SELLER: 45.

WOMAN: Sorry?

SELLER: 45.

WOMAN: 45. Can I try it, please?

SELLER: You can.

WOMAN: Thank you.

TAXI DRIVER: And apart from that you can do a bit of shopping too, shopping at Jalan Bukit Bintang where you have Lot 10 and the Jalan Bukit Bintang Plaza.

(*Scenes in the shopping centre*)

PASSENGER: What about handicrafts and things like that?

TAXI DRIVER: Handicrafts … let me see. You have some in the Central Market and there are some just around the Hilton. That's called Karyaneka.

(*Scenes at the handicrafts centre*)

TAXI DRIVER: And then there is the railway station which you should see in the daytime, and close to it also is the National Mosque, one of the biggest mosques and also where most official religious functions are held.

(*Shots of the railway station and National Mosque*)

PASSENGER: Are there lots of different kinds of restaurants?

TAXI DRIVER: Oh yes, this being a multi-racial country you have Chinese, Malay, Indian, Western food. They're always available all around town.

(*Scenes of restaurant at night*)

Part 3 Deborah Wildridge's visit

3.1 Haldo Developments – its products and markets

First view

1 Bollards (or street furniture);   2 All over the world

Second view

1 Managing Director;   2 street furniture;
3 local authorities; public utility companies, contractors

Videoscript

DEBORAH WILDRIDGE: My name is Deborah Wildridge and I'm the Managing Director of Haldo Developments Limited. Haldo Developments offer the world bollards – in a nutshell – which nobody ever understands the first time around, but it's street furniture, that's the technical term for it, and it's really products that are used on the roads. We sell in general to local authorities all over the world, sometimes to public utility companies and sometimes to contractors. But local authorities are our end users. And this part of the world is booming.

3.2 The value of the trade mission

First view

1 False. It is also for them to meet British people living in Malaysia.
2 False. She thinks they are very beneficial.
3 True.
4 True.

Second view

1 Because they can give advice on how to do business in Malaysia.
2 *experienced* and *generous*
3 Because it takes time for people to get to know you and trust you.

Videoscript

ERIC MATTEY: It's a trade reception and the purpose is for members of a British trade delegation to meet local contacts, not only Malaysian contacts but also British people living in Malaysia who have a good feel for how one goes about doing business in Malaysia.

DEBORAH WILDRIDGE: I think the trade missions are very beneficial. I find that travelling with a group of people – some of whom are very experienced – and they're very generous in sharing their knowledge and their experience. I'm very pleased with this trade mission.

ERIC MATTEY: They have to understand that doing business in the Far East, in Asia, is a lot different to doing business in traditional markets – Europe and North America.

DEBORAH WILDRIDGE: It takes time, it takes time in any market for us, but particularly I think it takes time in South-East Asia because you really need to get to know people and they need to get to know you, they need to trust you.

Language work

re<u>cep</u>tion	<u>gen</u>erous
<u>pur</u>pose	bene<u>fi</u>cial
dele<u>ga</u>tion	ex<u>per</u>ienced
<u>con</u>tacts	<u>know</u>ledge (the "k" is not pronounced)
<u>bus</u>iness (the "i" is not pronounced)	

3.3 Visiting a company

First view

1 Probably, they exchange business cards.
2 Yes, they were helpful and friendly.
3 In reception and the factory.

Second view

1 I;   2 have;   3 an;   4 appointment;   5 Welcome;   6 Let;   7 me;   8 most;
9 interesting;   10 be;   11 in;   12 touch;   13 get;   14 back

Videoscript

In reception

DEBORAH WILDRIDGE: Good morning. My name is Deborah Wildridge; I'm from Haldo Developments. I have an appointment with Mr Chua.

RECEPTIONIST: Can you take a seat first?

DEBORAH WILDRIDGE: Thank you.

RECEPTIONIST: (*on phone*) Mr Chua? Miss Debbie – Deborah is here to see you.

MR CHUA: Hello.

DEBORAH WILDRIDGE: Hello.

MR CHUA: Deborah? Welcome to Malaysia.

DEBORAH WILDRIDGE: Good morning. Thank you very much. This is my card.

MR CHUA: Here's mine.

DEBORAH WILDRIDGE: Thank you.

MR CHUA: Come, please come in.

DEBORAH WILDRIDGE: Thank you.

In the factory

MR CHUA: Let me show you. This is the metal we use – be careful! It's quite sharp. We use it for making our traffic signs.

DEBORAH WILDRIDGE: Uh, huh.

(*Deborah Wildridge is introduced by Mr Chua to a factory worker, who tells her about a resin they use in a manufacturing process*)

FACTORY WORKER: This is for Australia.

DEBORAH WILDRIDGE: And you import some from Korea?

FACTORY WORKER: Not from Korea, from Japan.

DEBORAH WILDRIDGE: From Japan?

FACTORY WORKER: From Japan.

At the end of the visit

DEBORAH WILDRIDGE: Good. Well, thank you very much indeed. It's been most interesting and I'll be in touch when I get back to England.

MR CHUA: We hope you enjoy your stay here and –

DEBORAH WILDRIDGE: Thank you very much.

MR CHUA: Please contact us if you need anything.

DEBORAH WILDRIDGE: Yes, I will do.

MR CHUA: Take care.

DEBORAH WILDRIDGE: Bye bye.

MR CHUA: Bye bye.

Language work

1 B is correct; A is too informal.
2 B is correct; A should be *would you mind taking a seat*.
3 B is correct; A is too direct to be polite.
4 B is correct; A is an order and not polite.
5 B is correct; A is too informal.
6 B is correct; A suggests there is a danger but *take care* is quite a usual way to end a conversation.

Practice 1

1 Roadtech;   2 morning;   3 factory;   4 signs;   5 contact;   6 distribute;   7 letter

Practice 2

Letter of thanks: model answer

Dear Mr Chua,
This is a short note to thank you for the warm welcome you gave me during my visit to your factory last week. I found the time most interesting. I do hope we shall be able to work together at some time in the future. Please do not hesitate to get in touch with me if there is any information you require.
With my best wishes,
Deborah Wildridge

Part 4 Malaysia – a changing country

4.1 How Kuala Lumpur has changed

First view

Kuala Lumpur has changed a lot.

Second view

1 was; 2 ago; 3 have; 4 arrived; 5 has; 6 since; 7 came; 8 is; 9 feel

Videoscript

YOONG KIM YENG: Well, Kuala Lumpur is very different from what it was ten years ago. Nowadays we have got many modern buildings, high rises and many modern facilities and amenities.

DEBORAH WILDRIDGE: I love to come back to KL. The second time I arrived it felt like coming home to some extent because I'm more familiar with the road system, where the buildings are. The skyline has changed completely in a year since I last came but I find it a very comfortable city to move around in, it's very easy. The food is delicious and I really feel at home this time.

Language work

1 Inflation has increased by just over 1% since 1995.
2 The number of women in government has gone up by 2.
3 Interest rates have fallen by roughly 1%.

4.2 Recent growth

First view

They both talk about how fast the Malaysian economy has grown.

Second view

1 1992; 2 51.5; 3 650%; 4 8; 5 5

Videoscript

YOONG KIM YENG: In terms of value of turnover, in 1992 we have a total of 51.5 billion ringgit. (In) 1993 it is 387.3 billion ringgit – an increase of 650%. The Kuala Lumpur stock exchange has grown from a small stock exchange to the largest stock exchange in South-East Asia.

ERIC MATTEY: The future for Malaysia is actually very exciting because the country has now been growing, the economy has been growing at about eight per cent for the last five years.

4.3 The future

First view

1 She hopes that Malaysia will not lose its cultural heritage.
2 Because they have a shortage of labour.

Second view

1 suppose; 2 much; 3 better; 4 standard; 5 of; 6 living;
7 low tech manufacturing; 8 higher; 9 necessary; 10 shortage

Videoscript

YOONG KIM YENG: I certainly hope that our people will not lose our cultural heritage by the year 2020 with the prosperity that comes along with it.

ERIC MATTEY: I suppose the benefit to the individual is they will have a much better standard of living. The changes in the country: I think we will see a move from low tech activity, manufacturing activity, to a much higher technological type of business which I think is necessary in Malaysia anyway because they have a shortage of labour.